THE
STRONGEST
WOMAN

*Through my
mother's eyes*

On a warm April's day as the flowers of spring were blooming, nestled in the heart of Orange County ,in New York's Hudson River Valley Region, near the Wallkill River and at the foothills of the Shawangunk Mountains ,in the year of our Lord, nineteen hundred and thirty eight, this story begins. The story of a strong woman, the strongest woman I know – my mother.   *Janie Sosa Gil*

Chapter One – The Fire

As I answered the phone, I could hear my brother's wavering voice, "There has been a fire," he said. We were both quiet for a moment that seemed like a lifetime. Both waiting for the other to speak, both afraid of what the other one would say. "Where?" I asked, almost afraid of the answer. "The cabin", His words seemed to echo as the tears ran down my face. My fear, my worst nightmare. The cabin was not safe, in fact it was a fire hazard. Our mother and stepfather lived there and my eight-year-old daughter. I was terrified. I knew this could not be good. All I could do was blurt out my daughter's name. Thank God she was okay, considering. She had suffered smoke inhalation and had cut her arm on the window and she was in shock. Sadly, Mom and Stepdad did not make it or two of the other grandchildren that had been in the house.

The windows of the cabin were exceedingly small. I had commented on it more than once. The furnace that heated the house was too close to the wall. But now it was too late. The pain in my heart took me to my knees and I cried out to God for help! I cannot do this by myself. "Where is my daughter?" I needed to get my daughter and bring her home. She had lived with my mother and stepfather for about six years. After going through a separation, I had left my daughter with them until I got on my feet, but when I went back for her my mother pleaded with me to let her stay for a little while longer which turned into six years. She had been taken to the hospital but thank God she was released the next day. I wanted to bring her home, but my younger sister opposed, saying that she needed time to adjust to the whole situation.

The days leading up to the funeral were agonizing. There were lots of questions. What happened? No one really knew. Did the furnace blow up? The furnace was in a new room that had been built on the side of the cabin. It was a bright room with many windows, a sunroom. It was here Momma received visitors. The rest of the rooms were much smaller and so were the windows.

I sat in front of the casket as the minister spoke, even though I could hear him, I could not listen. This all seemed like a nightmare and I was sure that at some point I would wake up. But this was not a bad dream, it was a reality. My mother was gone at forty-seven years old. My mind wondered back to 1943. I was six years old with two brothers and momma was expecting. I came home from school that early fall day to find that my mother was gone. I imagine I really did not know or obviously understand what was going on. Where was momma?
 My paternal grandmother was there but so were Social Services. One of my brothers and I were put in foster care. Grandma took the youngest. I was so sad. Where did momma go? What happened to her? No-one said anything. They got our things together and off we went. Thank God they kept my brother and I together. We were both scared, but neither of us dared to say or ask anything. An older lady kept us for a time. She would lock us in the basement and clothes pins were our toys. We stayed close by each other, almost as if we took refuge in each other. After a time, Grandma and our dad were able to get custody of us.

I was born into a low-income family in the Hudson River Valley New York. My father worked on the O&W Railroad, as did his father before him, and was a volunteer fireman. As a child he suffered scarlet fever. In his early years he put together a band and played Polkas around the area. One night playing a polka, and having had too much to drink, he was tied to the back of a pick-up truck, drug about 30 miles and left for dead. God chose to give him life. He was hospitalized for months and afterward could never use his left arm. He was never the same after that. "Pa" as everyone called him was an early riser. Every morning he was up at three, made his breakfast and took his daily walk.

I glanced back at the casket and realized the funeral service was ending. This was the most horrific day I had ever lived. I glanced at one of my younger sister. She had lost everything in that fire, father, mother and two children. I could not begin to comprehend how great her pain must be. I wanted to comfort her, but I had all I could do to hold myself up and deal with my own pain. The pallbearers lifted the small box that held all the remains, and we all made our way outside. It was a very cold March day, though the cold did not seem to affect me, I was numb. Snow and ice filled the streets and roads.

As we got into the cars and started up the mountain, my mind went back to the day my momma came home six years later. I was twelve years old, and coming home from school one day, I found a couple sitting with my grandmother in the kitchen. I did not know it at the time, but momma had been in an institution. My youngest brother was born there. Momma was her father's only child. She was a very strong-willed woman of German and Scandinavian Dutch descent with an angelic voice.   I did not recognize her but my grandmother calling me back into the kitchen said: "this is your mother" She had a new husband and later I found out she had two more daughters. I am not sure how I felt about it all, I guess I was numb then too.

I held back the tears as we made our way up the mountain. The hills were steep and the roads full of ice. I remembered going with my mom to the cabin for the first time. I was about thirteen and set in my ways. I must admit, I was not too happy with this new-found family I seemed to acquire.

Momma's new husband was a big, rough looking man; however, he was very gentle and loved my mother with all his heart. The cabin belonged to him and had been in his family for many years. He was widowed and had lived there with his first wife. The cabin was in a very secluded area. Even though there were other cabins nearby, they were all empty. I think it might have been a camp site at one time. It set quite far off the highway on a dirt road. A canal ran the whole length of the dirt road and deep into the woods that surrounded the cabin. There always seemed to be something about it that just did not set right with me.

The cemetery entrances were full of snow. The caretaker had obviously plowed but there was new fallen snow. As the many cars made their way in and around, I noticed that the last car was a police car. I pulled up to the site as best I could. My dad and grandmother had ridden with me. Grandma was eighty-four and had bad legs. I really did not want her to have to plow through the snow.

"Grandma", my father's mother, was a small, feisty woman of English and Scottish descent. Mother of three sons, she lost her husband when she was only thirty-six and never remarried. Her husband, my grandfather was killed on a hunting trip in the North Woods. It was said to have been a hunting accident, however everyone knew that had not been the case. Non the less it was left as that. Grandma and her sister Great Aunt Rene had cared for me and my brothers our whole life.

Great Aunt Rene had died only a few months before leaving a void in our lives. She too as her sister was a small framed, feisty woman, much thinner than Grandma though. She had died at eighty-six. Together these sisters had raised Grandma's three sons, my brothers and myself. As siblings they argued amongst themselves, but when Aunt Rene became sick, Grandma cared for her until her death.

As everyone made their way to the burial site, I could not hold back the tears any longer. It did not seem fair. I would never see my mother again. The minister finalized the ceremony, and the small casket was lowered into the ground. Everyone was so distraught; some people were screaming. I caught a glimpse of my daughter. I wanted to go to her and hold her, but I was afraid. We returned to our automobiles and as we drove away, I remembered the police car I had seen on our way in. As I pulled away, I looked through the rear-view mirror just in time to my see my brother getting out. He had been incarcerated at the time of the fire. The officers waited until everyone had left the grave site to let him out to at least pay his respects to a mother he would never see again.

Chapter Two – The Journey

When the county fair came to town that summer, I met a young man from Oklahoma. It was 1954, I had finished high school and I wanted to get away. There was a great big world out there and I wanted to see it. My newfound friend invited me to visit his family in Oklahoma and so I did. Oklahoma was quite different from New York. My friend's family were very soft-spoken country people. I did not stay long for fear of wearing out my welcome. The day I announced I would be leaving they pleaded with me to stay a while longer, but I felt it best to leave.

As I awaited, I saw the bus labeled "New Mexico" pull in. Glancing at my watch I realized it was almost quarter to one, the bus was running late. While boarding I caught a glimpse of three men sitting in the very end of the bus. For some reason they made me feel uncomfortable. Two older women sat in the seat across from me. A couple with two small children sat in the front seats and an older man was sitting behind me. Besides that, the bus was basically empty.

Close to six hours later the bus pulled into a small-town north of Santa Fe, NM. I was probably the first person off. I needed to get to the other side of the terminal to catch my second bus. I ran into the ladies' room but when I came out, I realized I had missed my bus. I did not know what to do, so I set out on the road. It all happened so fast that before I could even scream, I had been pulled into a car   It was the worst experience I had ever had. I really did not have anything of value, but they took my watch none the less. They opened the door, pushed me out of the car and pulled away, leaving me alongside of the road. Obviously, they were from the area. I thought of looking for a policeman but what could they do. The men were already gone. They had covered my face so I really could not identify them. Besides, all I wanted was to get as far away from that place as possible. I felt like I wanted to die.

I got my things as I tried to pull myself together. They had opened my suitcase looking for valuables. I continued to walk until I came to a rest stop where I tried to clean up before getting the bus that would take me on my journey. I was hurt, physically, but much more emotionally. Thankfully, they did not take the little money I had, but they took something much more valuable and worthier, my shame and self-esteem. I realized God had kept me. I tried to think good thoughts, yet the picture of those men played over and over in my mind.

The bus finally pulled away, next stop San Diego, California. This time the bus was full capacity. It seemed like every seat was taken. It was late at night, so everyone was quiet. I think I was suffering from exhaustion and just collapsed in my seat. This bus would take me into San Diego, although there would be some stops along the way. It was estimated to be approximately 15 hours. I slept right through the Phoenix Arizona stop and woke up about twenty minutes later. We were only about eight hours into the trip. I was hungry but I was afraid to get off the bus and besides, I was scarce on money. When I awoke, I realized that the older lady that had been sitting next to me was no longer there. Now there was a much younger woman with a little boy, who was in the seat on the other side of the isle. She was having some difficulty tending to the little guy, so I offered to change seats with him. As we continued our journey, the young woman sparked up a conversation. She had been visiting relatives in Phoenix and was now on her way home to San Diego. She seemed very pleasant and it did me good to get my mind off my misfortune.

She explained that she was recently divorced and was starting a new job. Her son had been staying with family in Phoenix while she got back on her feet after the divorce. Now she would need someone to care for him while she worked. By the time the bus rolled into San Diego, about 11 hours later, I had agreed to stay with her, at least for the time being. She needed someone to care for her son and I needed a place to stay.

I was grateful for this opportunity. I do not think I would have made it if I would have had to stay in the street.

Her apartment was small, but she gave me my own room. She occupied the bigger bedroom with her son. Room and board and a few dollars extra. That works, I thought. I was alone with the child most of the time. I cleaned up and cooked, it was the least I could do. San Diego was quite different from New York and undoubtedly from Oklahoma. There was much prejudice. I really felt like I did not belong.

I had a lot of time on my hands while the child slept, and I began to write. It was a story about my journey, my life. It did not take long to write, but then what. It was extremely hard to get a book published in those days. The woman I worked for said the story was good and that she knew some people. Trustingly, I handed her my story. Some months later the story was published, but not under my name. She said that since I was under eighteen, the book had been published in her name. There was nothing I could do. It took some time but eventually I realized that the grass is not always greener on the other side. I called my mother and she sent me the money to come home

Chapter Three - Happily Ever After

As I watched my brother through the rear view mirror my heart saddened even more and tears rolled down my face. I wanted to stop and turn around, just to be able to put my arms around him, but I knew I could not, the sheriff would not allow it. I obviously did not want to create a problem, so I continued. I motioned to my dad and he looked back to get a glimpse of his eldest son. This family has surely had its share of grief.

After returning home from my journey to Oklahoma and San Diego, Ca. I went to work waiting on tables in a Bowling Alley. There I met a young man who had been in the Korean War. He was so handsome; I fell head over heels for him. Not long after we were married, and he took me to New York City to his aunt's house; but things did not go well, and I returned home. Our on, off relationship lasted about three years, and God blessed us with two beautiful daughters.

In one last attempt to make our relationship work, we moved to Newark, New Jersey to a small studio apartment with our oldest daughter. But things were too far gone, no matter how we tried it did not work out and I finally found myself alone with my girls. After a time, I entered a second relationship.

I pulled out of the cemetery following the procession of automobiles. If the roads were dangerous going up the mountain, much more so going down. This was real country out here, I thought. I tried to concentrate on our journey down the mountain. The roads were very narrow and winding. Because of the snow and ice, they were very slippery and dangerous. I kept thinking about my brother. As a boy he had been wrongfully accused of stealing and had been sent away. It seems like life had not treated him very well. Now as an adult he was incarcerated. I hoped I would see him again soon. I loved my brothers and sisters. My mind went back to my daughter. My youngest sister had taken her, but she was my daughter and I wanted and needed to bring her home.

I was only twenty-eight at the time and had five children. My two daughters from my first relationship, and a son and two more daughters from my second. The youngest three lived with their father and maternal grandmother. I had tried to get my children back but had not succeeded. I do not think we are ever ready for the things and situations life throws at us. I am sure no one sets out in life preparing for the worst, but unfortunately sometimes that is the hand they are dealt – the worst. Searching my thoughts, I realized that none of us seemed to have that "happy ever after" My parents' marriage was not a happy one and probably were not together more than seven years. My father loved my mother, perhaps up until the day she died. He never re-married. But he dealt with many issues.

I wanted that "happy ever after" and so I went through many relationships, seeking that "happy ever after", what I never seemed to find. I worked hard and did all I could for my children, even though none of them lived with me. In 1968, I returned to my grandmother's house where my two oldest girls lived. I felt stable. I taught myself Spanish and besides my regular job, helped many as an interpreter.

As we continued down the mountain, I thought, "what now"? The fire seemed to cause friction amongst the siblings. Many people speculated if it had been an accident or arson.

As a child and young teen my dad always took me to church and so I had some knowledge of God. However, in my later life I lived far from Him. My daughters went to church with a neighbor family and in 1977 I began to visit on Sundays. One Sunday night during the service, I received the baptism of The Holy Spirit. I had never experienced anything so wonderful before, my life was changed! I began to serve God with all my heart. I knew that only God had brought me through everything life had thrown my way. I had issues to fix but I left it all in God's hands. Jesus had found me, and I never wanted Him to let me go!

As the years went by, no one ever spoke of the fire again. No investigation, everything was just let as is, even though I believe it was always in the back of everyone's mind. My dad had suffered a stroke and in 1979 died. I believe he loved my mother until his last breath. Grandma had left us in 1972 also after a stroke. My oldest daughter had married and in 1979, just a few months before my dad passed, moved thousands of miles away from me, taking my two oldest grandsons. I was so close to them and no longer having them close by really hurt. A couple of years later, I once again left my hometown, moving to New Jersey.

Life was quite different. The family patriarchs and matriarchs were no longer with us. All my children were grown and had made their own lives. I was happy in the Lord teaching Sunday School and singing in the choir. I began working a new job and not long after I met someone, and for a split second, I took my eyes off Jesus and my world turned upside down. I cannot even begin to tell you what a mistake that was. I lost everything, my marriage, my position in church, my home. It only takes one split second to fall, one split second to lose everything, one split second to lose the most valuable thing, your relationship with Jesus. My children were angry with me, but I knew that Jesus still loved me. After a time, He found me again. He helped me to find my way home to Him. He had never left me; it had been me who left Him.

As I look back over the years one thing is true, God has never left me. All through His Word God promises to never leave us or forsake us, and He is true to His Word and promises.

"Be strong and courageous. Do not be afraid or terrified because of them, for the Lord your God goes with you; He will never leave you or forsake you." Deut. 31:6 (NIV)

"Keep your life free from love of money, and be content with what you have, for He has said, "I will never leave you nor forsake you." Heb 13:5 (ESV)

Many times I remember my mother and the fire, and I cannot help but think that everything would have been different had she not left that fall day in 1943. I remember my dad not speaking for over a year after suffering his first stroke. He needed surgery and my youngest daughter, and I waited with him. I stepped out of the room for a moment and my daughter prayed that he would speak. As I entered the room my Dad spoke my name. He never spoke again. Not long after he suffered a second stroke and went home with the Lord. I remember Grandma and Great Aunt Rene and how they loved us and cared for us and I thank God for having had them in our lives.

Chapter Five – Through My Mother's Eyes

On a warm April's day as the flowers of spring were blooming, nestled in the heart of Orange County ,in New York's Hudson River Valley Region, near the Wallkill River and at the foothills of the Shawangunk Mountains ,in the year of our Lord, nineteen hundred and thirty eight, this story begins. The story of a strong woman, the strongest woman I know – my mother.

I would have to say that at eleven one really does not know about suffering or strength. One does not know much about death, but this was the second time in less than a year that our family had dealt with death. As we sat in the funeral service my eleven-year-old eyes were fixated on my mother's face. My mother's eyes told the story of the pain which seemed too much for her to bear.

 But my mother is a strong woman, the strongest woman I know, much stronger than I. Throughout my life I have watched this strong woman. When I lived thousands of miles away, a phone call from her seemed to make everything better. She has dried my tears, made me laugh and has always been there for me. She began working at an early age and was a hard worker. From Shop Steward, to machine operator, to secretarial work, waiting tables, construction company owner, construction worker and interpreter. Having a love to travel, she has traveled throughout most of the continental United States, Puerto Rico, and Nicaragua,

Guatemala, and Costa Rica, and has made tons of road trips, near and far.

But her greatest love of all, is her love for Jesus. She has never been ashamed of the Gospel of Jesus Christ or her love for Him. She has been a faithful witness of the Gospel, without fear to share her faith and testimony with others. She has been blessed with an angelic voice and has always glorified God in song and worship.

On her eighty first birthday, she was hospitalized with a bacterial infection in her blood stream. She needed many weeks of antibiotics and during her hospital stay was given a pacemaker.
Today, I am her caregiver. At eighty-two she walks a little slower and her mind is not as swift as it used to be. One thing has not changed though, her love for her family and her love for the King of kings and Lord of lords. No matter how difficult situations might seem, she always says that God has promised to never leave or forsake us.

Fifty-three years have passed since the fire and no one really ever speaks about it, it is still too painful even after all this time. Still we lovingly remember those that have gone on before us, the patriarchs, and matriarchs of the family. Today, mom is the matriarch and her brothers the patriarchs and should the Lord tarry, one day my generation, will be in their place.

Most of her days are spent resting especially now during the pandemic of COVID-19 that we are currently living. But still God is good! He has given her many days!

"I believe that I shall look upon the goodness of the Lord in the land of the living! Wait for the Lord; be strong and let your heart take courage; wait for the Lord!"

Psalms 27:13,14 (ESV)

This book is being dedicated to the four people that lost their lives in   "The Fire"

John and Mary   Michael and Diana

             and to the three survivors

Catherine   Debra   Veronica

Special thanks to:

     Debra Sosa, Christina Ellis, Sara Castillo

STRONG WOMEN OF FAITH

Abigail – The Peacemaker

1 Sam 25:23" When Abigail saw David, she hurried and got down from the donkey and fell before David on her face and bowed to the ground." (ESV)

This woman whom the Bible calls, discerning and beautiful, intervened and brought peace to the situation when her husband Nabal, a harsh and badly behaved man disrespected David the future king. After Nabal's death, Abigail became King David's wife

Help us Lord to be like Abigail, sowers of peace

Jochebed – The Selfless Woman

Exodus 2:3 "When she could hide him no longer, she took for him a basket made with papyrus and covered it with tar and pitch. Then she put the child in it and set it among the reeds by the bank of the Nile." (AMP)

This woman was the mother of Moses who was born at a time when all male Hebrew children were ordered to be killed upon birth. Jochebed hid her child for three months, until it became impossible. When she could hide him no longer, she took a basket, made it waterproof, put her child in it and set in in the Nile River. Jochebed showed great faith in God in doing this. She put her son's needs before her own. Moses became the great deliverer of the Hebrew nation.

Help us Lord to put others needs before our own.

Ruth – The Friend

Ruth 1:16: But Ruth said, "Do not urge me to leave you or to return from following you. For where you go, I will go, and where you live, I will live. Your people shall be my people and your God my God."

This woman whose name in Hebrew means "**friend**" truly was a true friend, a faithful friend to her mother in law, a woman aged and alone. Ruth left everything, family, country, customs', all that she knew to selflessly follow Naomi to an unknown land and an unknown people, aware that Naomi had nothing to offer her. Ruth is a true example of what a real friend is.

Help us Lord to be a true friend

Deborah – The Warrior

Judges 4:8,9 – " If you go with me I will go, but if you will not go with me, I will not go. And she said, I will surely go."

Deborah was the only female judge of the Israelites. Not only was she a judge, but also a prophetess. The Bible tells us in the Book of Judges that due to their disobedience and evil ways the children of Israel had been given over to their enemies, Jabin king of Canaan and the commander of his army, Sisera, who cruelly oppressed the Israelites for twenty years.

And God commanded Barak to take up an army and go after Sisera. In the portion we read in the beginning, Barak tells Deborah, "if you go with me, I will go, but if you will not go with me, I will not go." Deborah answered in verse 9" I will surely go"

Besides being a judge and prophetess, Deborah was also a warrior. Deborah did not fear the enemy, she had a Word! God had promised to turn the enemy over to them and that He did. God is a God of promise, a faithful God.

Deborah did not fear the enemy because she was a warrior, and she knew that God was on her side.

Help us Lord to be warriors full of faith and trust to hold on to the Word we have received.

From the memoires of Ruth M Newhall as told to

Janie Sosa Gil - Author

Janie Sosa Gil - Author